MAMMALS

Gray Wolf
Canis lupus To 6.5 ft. (2 m)
Coat color is usually gray, but black, white and mottled variants exist. Attacks on humans are rare, but packs have killed handlers when in captivity.

Mountain Lion
Puma concolor
To 9 ft. (2.7 m)
Reclusive species is found in mountainous regions throughout western North America. Occasionally attacks humans, usually small children.

Elk
Cervus canadensis To 10 ft. (3 m)
Elk are resident pests in many Rocky Mountain towns. During the fall rutting season, males are very irritable and will charge humans and vehicles unprovoked.

Moose
Alces alces To 10 ft. (3 m)
Will spontaneously charge when threatened and attempt to gore and trample the threat. Have been known to charge vehicles and, in one instance, killed the occupant.

Most animal attacks are a result of human carelessness. Rarely do large animals treat humans as a food source. The ones that do attack tend to circle their prey with their ears pinned back trying to determine the method of attack. NEVER RUN from a potentially dangerous animal as this will trigger its attack instinct. Make yourself appear as large as possible and back away while talking in an audible, low voice. If the animal does attack, fight back with all your might, aiming for sensitive areas such as the nose and eyes.

This guide identifies some of the most feared and dangerous North American species of animals and plants. The purpose of the guide is twofold: 1) to debunk irrational myths about species such as snakes, spiders, sharks and bears; 2) to educate people about the proper action to take if one is confronted and/or injured by these dangerous species.

N.B. – The publisher makes no representation or warranties with respect to the accuracy, completeness, correctness or usefulness of this information and specifically disclaims any implied warranties of fitness for a particular purpose. The advice, strategies and/or techniques contained herein may not be suitable for all individuals. The publisher shall not be responsible for any physical harm (up to and including death), loss of profit or other commercial damage. The publisher assumes no liability brought or instituted by individuals or organizations arising out of or relating in any way to the application and/or use of the information, advice and strategies contained herein.

Made in the USA

Waterford Press produces reference guides that introduce novices to nature, science, travel and recreation. Product information is featured on the website:
www.waterfordpress.com

Text and illustrations © 2006, 2020 by Waterford Press Inc. All rights reserved. Cover images © iStock Photo. To order, call 800-434-2555. For permissions, or to share comments, e-mail editor@waterfordpress.com. For information on custom-published products, call 800-434-2555 or e-mail info@waterfordpress.com.

ISBN 978-1-58355-309-1 $7.95 U.S.
50795
9 781583 553091
UPC
8 84682 00951 9
10 9 8 7 6 5 4 3 2 205207

DANGEROUS ANIMALS & PLANTS

Kavanagh/Leung

A POCKET NATURALIST® GUIDE

DANGEROUS ANIMALS & PLANTS

A Folding Pocket Guide to Dangerous North American Species

T0123967

POISONOUS PLANTS

The following plants all contain toxic compounds that can cause illness, and even death, if consumed. Most are toxic to humans and their pets.

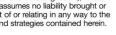

Buckeye
Aesculus spp. To 30 ft. (9 m)
Pinkish flowers bloom in erect clusters in spring. Large seeds have a light 'eye' spot. All parts of the plant are toxic.

Coralbean
Erythrina spp. To 25 ft. (7.5 m)
Branches have stout, curved thorns. Distinctive elongate scarlet flowers bloom in a showy spike and are succeeded by pods containing poisonous red seeds.

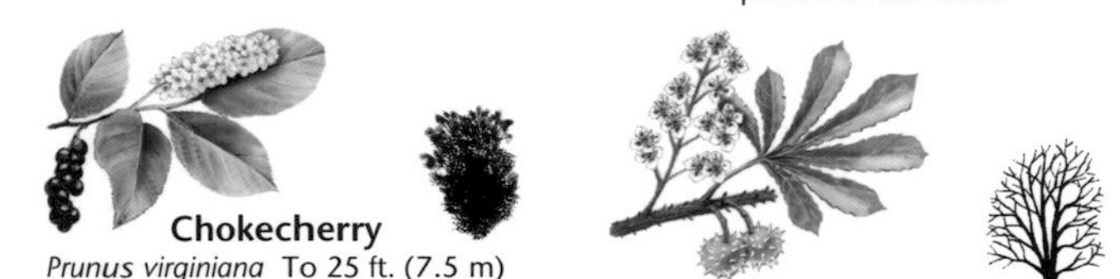

Chokecherry
Prunus virginiana To 25 ft. (7.5 m)
Cylindrical clusters of spring flowers are succeeded by dark red-purple berries. Edible pea-sized fruits are extremely tart. Fruit pits and wilted leaves contain a weak cyanide.

Horse Chestnut
Aesculus hippocastanum To 50 ft. (15 m)
Small flowers are succeeded by spiny green 'balls'. Seeds are poisonous. Common in towns and landscaped areas.

Buttercup
Ranunculus spp.
To 10 in. (25 cm)
Flowers have glossy petals that are not notched. All parts of the plant contain toxic or irritating oils.

Mayapple
Podophyllum peltatum
To 20 in. (50 cm)
Cup-shaped flowers bloom between 2 leaves. The seeds, leaves and roots are poisonous.

Jimsonweed
Datura spp.
To 5 ft. (1.5 m)
Large white flowers are trumpet-shaped. All parts of the plant are poisonous.

Locoweed
Oxytopis spp.
To 10 in. (25 cm)
Plant has pea-shaped yellow, cream, purple or reddish flowers. All parts of plant are poisonous.

Death Camas
Zigadenus elegans
To 3 ft. (90 cm)
Star-shaped, green-centered flowers bloom in a long cluster. Leaves are grass-like. All parts of plant are deadly poisonous.

Larkspur
Delphinium spp.
To 6 ft. (1.8 m)
5-part blue to white flowers have prominent spurs. Often blamed for poisoning livestock.

Foxglove
Digitalis purpurea
To 5 ft. (1.5 m)
Distinctive hanging purple-pink flowers bloom along stem. All parts of the plant are poisonous.

POISONOUS PLANTS

Water Hemlock
Cicuta maculata
To 7 ft. (2.1 m)
Wetland plant has flat-topped clusters of white flowers. Leaves are sharply toothed. All parts of the plant are poisonous.

Red and White Baneberry
Actaea rubra
To 3 ft. (90 cm)
Flowers bloom in a dense conical cluster and are succeeded by poisonous red berries in summer.

Poison Hemlock
Conium maculatum
To 10 ft. (3 m)
Purple-spotted stems have distinct ridges. Leaves are parsley-like. Flowers bloom in flat-topped clusters. All parts of the plant are deadly poisonous.

Monkshood
Aconitum columbianum
To 6 ft. (1.8 m)
Deep blue flowers resemble a monk's habit. All parts of the plant are deadly poisonous.

Nightshade
Solanum spp.
Stems to 10 ft. (3 m) long. Vine or leafy plant has purplish star-shaped flowers with a yellow 'beak' of protruding stamens. Foliage and fruit are poisonous.

Rhododendron (Azalea)
Rhododendron spp.
To 25 ft. (7.5 m)
Flowering shrub has showy pink, white or orange blossoms. All parts of the plant are poisonous.

Poison Ivy
Toxicodendron radicans
To 100 ft. (30 m)
3-part leaves turn red in autumn. The similar poison oak (*T. diversilobum*) has 3-part, oak-like leaflets.

Lantana
Lantana camara
To 40 in. (1 m)
Flowers are arranged in an outer and inner ring. The leaves and unripe fruits are poisonous.

Giant Hogweed
Heracleum mantegazzianum
To 25 ft. (7.6 m)
Compound leaves are up to 4 ft. (1.2 m) wide. White flowers bloom in dense clusters. The plant secretes a toxin that causes severe blistering and can cause blindness.

Wild Parsnip
Pastinaca sativa
To 5 ft. (1.5 m)
Large plant has flat clusters of small yellow flowers. Plant saps can cause severe rashes and burns.

CONTACT POISON RASHES

Symptoms include burning, reddening, itching, swelling and blistering and may take hours or even days to appear. The effects are spread by scratching and the oil can also get on gear which will infect whoever touches it. When symptoms first appear, it is recommended to wash the affected area with water repeatedly. If water is not readily available, use dirt or sand to remove the oil from the skin.

MUSHROOMS

As a rule, novices should NEVER consume a wild mushroom unless they consult an expert to ensure positive identification. Over 200 North American species are poisonous and 10 or more are deadly. Experienced mushroom collectors have died by consuming mis-identified species. Even in a survival situation, mushrooms should be avoided since they have little nutritional value.

Destroying Angel
Amanita virosa
To 10 in. (25 cm)
Cap: White, smooth.
Stalk: Basal bulb, collar.
Habitat: Mixed forests.

Death Cap
Amanita phalloides
To 5 in. (13 cm)
Cap: Smooth, greenish-yellow or yellow-brown.
Stalk: Basal bulb, collar.
Habitat: Woodlands, especially under oaks and conifers.

Fly Agaric
Amanita muscaria
To 7 in. (18 cm)
Cap: Yellow to red-orange cap has white warts.
Stalk: Basal bulb, collar.
Habitat: Oak and coniferous forests.

Panther
Amanita pantherina
To 4 in. (10 cm)
Cap: Brown to yellow with light warts.
Stalk: Basal bulb, collar.
Habitat: Coniferous forests.

Witch's Hat
Hygrophorus conicus
To 8 in. (20 cm)
Cap: Red-orange, conical.
Stalk: Faint longitudinal lines.
Habitat: Coniferous forests.

Scaly Pholiota
Pholiota squarrosa
To 4 in. (10 cm)
Cap: Yellow-brown, covered with pointy dark scales.
Stalk: Scaly like cap.
Habitat: Deciduous and coniferous forests.

Jack O'Lantern
Omphalotus olearius
To 8 in. (20 cm)
Cap: Yellow to orange.
Stalk: Same color as cap.
Habitat: Oak and mixed forests. Malodorous, often grows in clusters on stumps and roots.

Emetic Russula
Russula emetica
To 4 in. (10 cm)
Cap: Red, shiny, edges are ridged.
Stalk: White, smooth.
Habitat: Swampy areas, mixed woods.

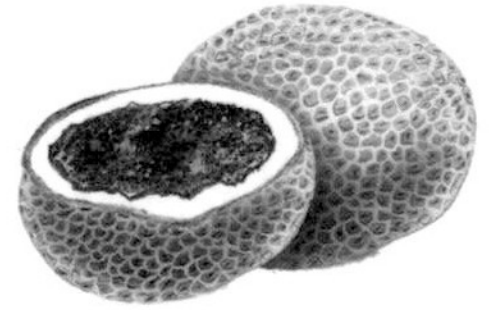

Poison Puffball
Scleroderma aurantium
To 4 in. (10 cm) wide.
Description: Warty, yellow-brown ball contains blackish spores when mature. Rind is white.
Habitat: Grassy areas, woodlands.

PLANT POISONINGS

Seek medical help immediately. Remove any plant parts from the victim's mouth. If they are not breathing, call 9-1-1. Try to determine what plant parts were ingested and when. Bring samples of all plant parts with you to the emergency room. Acting quickly could save a victim's life.

DANGEROUS NEARSHORE CREATURES

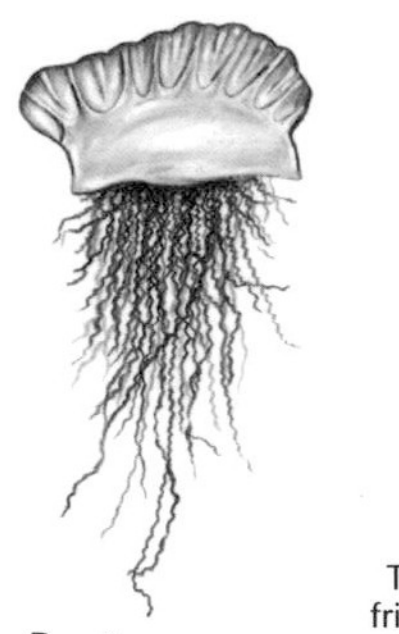

Portuguese Man-of-War
Physalia physalis
Float to 12 in. (30 cm) long.
Common in the Gulf Stream. Tentacles pack a powerful sting that can affect breathing and motor skills.

Moon Jellyfish
Aurelia aurita
To 16 in. (40 cm)
Translucent jellyfish has a fringe of stinging tentacles. Commonly washed up on beaches after storms. Stingers can still be active even if the animal is dead.

Lion's Mane Jellyfish
Cyanea capillata
Float to 8 ft. (2.4 m) long. The world's largest jellyfish has a highly toxic sting that causes blistering and burning.

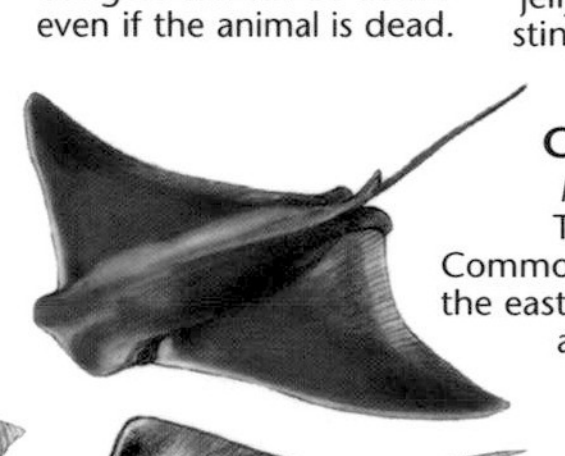

Cownose Ray
Rhinoptera spp.
To 3 ft. (90 cm)
Common in shallow waters in the east. Tail spines can cause a painful injury.

Cone Shell
Conus spp.
To 3 in. (8 cm)
Sub-tropical mollusk shoots a toxic dagger out of the narrow end of the shell. Wounds can cause paralysis and death if untreated.

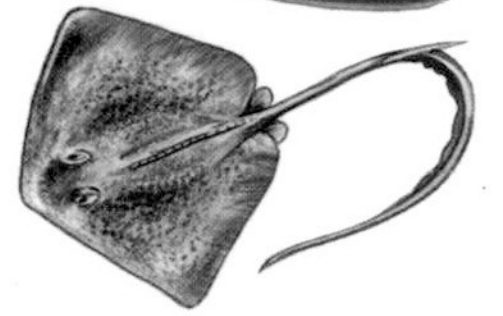

Stingray
Dasyatis spp.
To 3 ft. (90 cm)
Has a thin, whip-like tail with one or more barbed spines that can inflict painful wounds.

Long-spined Sea Urchin
Diadema antillarium
Body to 4 in. (10 cm)
Reef-dweller is protected by poisonous spines up to 6 in. (15 cm) long.

FISHES THAT ARE POISONOUS TO EAT

The flesh or organs of these species are poisonous to consume. Note that any species of fish can be toxic if it comes from contaminated waters.

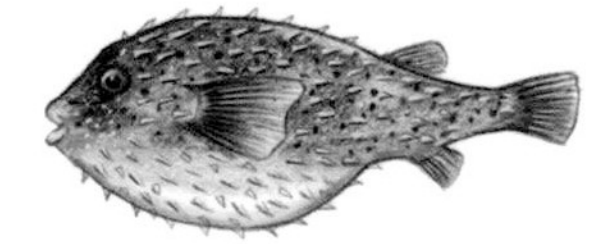

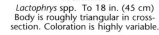

Porcupinefish
Diodon hystrix To 2 ft. (60 cm)
Inflates itself into a spiny ball when threatened. Flesh is poisonous.

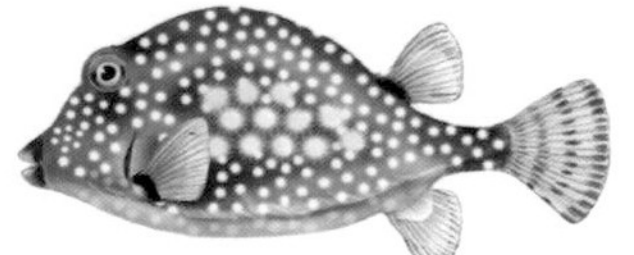

Trunkfish
Lactophrys spp. To 18 in. (45 cm)
Body is roughly triangular in cross-section. Coloration is highly variable.

Triggerfish
Balistes spp. To 19 in. (48 cm)
Highly variable group of fishes have parrot-like mouths.

Pufferfish
Sphoeroides spp. To 14 in. (35 cm)
Inflates body as a means of defense. Flesh is extremely poisonous.

FLYING INSECTS

Many flying insects sting when threatened. For most people, stings typically cause redness, swelling and a mild headache that passes in a few hours. Those who are allergic to venom can have severe reactions including anaphalactic shock, coma and death. Symptoms of allergic reactions include shortness of breath, nausea, vomiting and swelling around the nose and mouth. Get victim medical help IMMEDIATELY. Insect stings kill 50-100 people each year in North America.

Hornet (Yellowjacket)
Vespula spp.
To .6 in. (1.8 cm)
Black and yellow banded picnic pests will sting repeatedly when threatened.

Bumble Bee
Bombus spp.
To .75 in. (1.8 cm)
Stout, furry bee is large and noisy. Sting injects venom into victim. Unlike the honey bee, can sting repeatedly.

Killer Bee (Africanized Honey Bee)
Apis mellifera
To .8 in. (2 cm)
Red-brown insect has yellowish rings on its shiny abdomen. Can sting only once and leaves a barbed stinger and poison sac attached to its victim. This is an extremely aggressive form of honey bee that will attack a perceived threat with excessive force. Swarms of these bees have caused a number of human fatalities.

Carpenter Bee
Xylocopa spp.
To 1 in. (3 cm)
Large, bumblebee-like insect has a smooth, blackish abdomen. Non-stinging male has a white spot on its face.

Paper Wasp
Polistes spp.
To 1 in. (3 cm)
Told by slender profile and dark, pale-banded abdomen. Builds hanging, papery nests. Inflicts a painful sting.

Black Horsefly
Tabanus atratus
To 1 in. (3 cm)
Note large head. Female feeds on blood and delivers painful bites. The similar deerfly has dark-patterned wings.

Mosquito
Family Culicidae
To .25 in. (.6 cm)
Slender, disease-spreading insect has shiny, blood-sucking beak. Responsible for more deaths worldwide than any other animal.

HOW TO AVOID BEING STUNG

The best tactic for self-protection is avoidance. Avoid areas where bees are feeding on flowers. Meat-eating hornets are attracted to strong food smells, so avoid picnicking on pungent meats like fish in their vicinity. Avoid wearing attractants such as perfume or cologne or brightly colored clothing.

IF YOU ARE ATTACKED

Run away from swarm and seek shelter in an automobile or building. If no shelter is available, keep running. If you are being stung, cover your eyes, nose and mouth with your arms or a piece of clothing. Do not flail your arms or attack the bees – especially killer bees – since this will cause them to intensify their attack.

BITES & STINGS

Bee stingers should be removed as quickly as possible by stroking them out with a knife, credit card or fingernail. Do not squeeze poison sac at end of honey bee stinger since this will inject more venom. Black widow spider bites, fiddleback spider bites and scorpion stings can be fatal (especially to children) if left untreated. Seek medical attention immediately. It is always advisable to apply a cold compress to a sting wound to slow blood flow and decrease swelling.

SPIDERS & SCORPIONS

All four have four pairs of segmented legs. Many weave webs to capture prey while others pounce on their victims. Some species have a venomous bite used to immobilize their prey.

Tarantula
Family Theraphosidae
To 3 in. (8 cm)
Large hairy spider. Prominent fangs can inflict a painful bite. Venom is mild.

Black Widow Spider
Latrodectus mactans
To .3 in. (8 mm)
Black spider is easily recognized by its shiny, bulbous abdomen with a red hourglass marking. Venom can be lethal to children and the elderly. There are roughly 2,500 reported black widow bites every year in the United States. Bites generally cause severe pain and muscle cramping.

Fiddleback Spider
Loxosceles reclusa
To .4 in. (11 mm)
Easily distinguished by violin-shaped marking on its back. Bites cause tissue degeneration.

Scorpion
Order Scorpionida To 5 in. (13 cm)
Lobster-like creature has a long tail with a stinger at the tip. Common in warm dry climates. Sting is potentially fatal to children and the elderly.

TICKS, ANTS, ETC.

Actual size

Tick
Dermacentor spp.
To .25 in. (6 mm)
Small blood-sucking insects inhabit forested and grassy areas. They are dangerous to humans because they transmit diseases including Lyme's disease and encephalitis. Because ticks take at least 6 hours to transmit the diseases to their host, taking the time to do regular 'tick checks' while hiking is an effective preventative measure. DO NOT attempt to remove by simply pulling on the body or head may remain embedded. Use heat, gas, alcohol, hot water or petroleum jelly to make it back out. Insect repellent is an effective preventative measure.

Fire Ant
Solenopsis geminata
To .3 in. (8 mm)
Dull red, yellow or black ant is named for its burning sting. Stings can cause shortness of breath, dizziness and even anaphalactic shock in sensitive victims.

Pond Leech
Macrobdella spp.
To 10 in. (25 cm)
Worm-like creature has red or black spots down its side. Common in ponds, lakes, swamps and stagnant water. Attaches to the skin with suckers, makes a small lesion, and feeds on blood. Often a source of infections. Do not attempt to remove forcibly as this can increase risk of infection. Apply salt or heat to its body to make it release.

Velvet-Ant
Family Mutillidae
To 1 in. (3 cm)
Furry wasp scurries about on the ground like an ant. Usually brightly colored red, yellow or orange. Bite packs a powerful sting.

Common House Centipede
Order Chilopoda
To 4 in. (10 cm)
Has a single pair of legs per segment and long antennae. Can inflict a painful, venomous bite, though consequences are seldom serious.

SHARKS

This group includes the most feared predators of the sea. They've caused an average of one death a year in the USA over the past 10 years. It is more likely you will get hit by a piece of falling space junk than be bitten by a shark. These four species account for most human casualties.

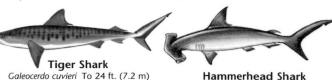

Tiger Shark
Galeocerdo cuvieri To 24 ft. (7.2 m)
Has a short snout, sides are covered with dark blotches. Highly aggressive.

Hammerhead Shark
Sphyrna mokarran To 20 ft. (6 m)
Responsible for the majority of attacks in North American waters.

Great White Shark
Carcharodon carcharias To 21 ft. (6.4 m)
Robust, blunt-nosed shark is gray above and white below. Found in temperate and cold coastal waters worldwide.

Mako Shark
Isurus spp. To 14 ft. (4.2 m)
Sharp-snouted shark is blue to gray above and white below. Common in temperate waters.

SHARK SMARTS

Sharks are attracted by weak vibration (e.g., wounded fish) and smell (blood, body waste and garbage). They are repelled by strong vibration. Individuals are more vulnerable than groups. Groups should bunch together, face outward, and energetically kick at and slap the water's surface to deter shark. If you have a knife, aim for the eyes, gills, or try to stab it in the brain.

FISHES

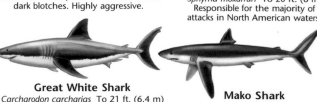

Green Moray
Gymnothorax funebris To 6 ft. (1.8 m)
Stocky eel has a long dorsal and anal fin and toothy jaws. Common in shallow coral reefs. Can become aggressive if provoked.

Stonecat
Noturus flavus To 12 in. (30 cm)
Has white blotches at base of dorsal fin and on upper edge of unforked tail. Like all North American catfishes, it has 4 pairs of mouth barbels and a sharp spine on each dorsal and pectoral fin. The stonecat's pectoral spines are venomous.

Barracuda
Sphyraena spp. To 4 ft. (1.2 m)
Slender, silvery fish has jutting lower jaw and prominent, blade-like teeth. Barracudas are aggressive predators and have been known to attack divers without provocation. Flesh is poisonous.

Northern Pike
Esox lucius To 53 in. (1.3 m)
Note large head and posterior dorsal fin. Large pike have been known to bite small children.

Swordfish
Xiphias gladius To 14 ft. (4.2 m)
Has long, flattened bill and short-based dorsal fin. Has been known to attack boats.

Varied group of snakes all have spade-shaped heads and a tail rattle that they shake when threatened. Will bite when threatened. They kill between 5-15 people in North America each year. 15 North American species.

RATTLESNAKES

Western Diamondback Rattlesnake
Crotalus atrox To 7 ft. (2.1 m)
Has a row of light-bordered dark diamonds down its back. Also called coon-tailed rattler, its tail is banded in black-and-white.

Timber Rattlesnake
Crotalus horridus To 6 ft. (1.8 m)
Note dark and light bands down body and black tail.

COPPERHEADS

Usually responsible for the most venomous bites in the U.S. annually. Rarely fatal. 5 North American subspecies.

Copperhead
Agkistrodon contortrix To 52 in. (1.3 m)
Has hourglass-shaped bands down its back. Color varies from copper to orange to pinkish.

COTTONMOUTHS

Fat-bodied aquatic snakes are very aggressive if disturbed. Bites cause tissue damage that can lead to amputation if untreated. 3 North American subspecies.

Cottonmouth
Agkistrodon piscivorus To 6 ft. (1.8 m)
Large water snake has a spade-shaped head. When threatened, it snaps its mouth open revealing the white lining inside.

CORAL SNAKES

Slender snakes have a very small mouth and are usually harmless unless handled. Venom is extremely toxic and bites can be fatal. Remember the maxim, 'Red on yellow can kill a fellow'. 2 North American species.

Eastern Coral Snake
Micrurus fulvius
To 4 ft. (1.2 m)
Red, black and yellow snake has a black nose. Note red bands touch yellow bands.

Scarlet Kingsnake
Lampropeltis triangulum
To 6.5 ft. (2 m)
One of several harmless snakes that mimic the coloration of the coral snake. Note red nose and that red bands never touch yellow bands.

SNAKE BITES

The bite from a poisonous snake usually causes a burning sensation in the affected area, followed by swelling and discoloration. Most venomous snakes inject the venom. It is not advisable to cut the wound and try to suck out the poison since this will only cause the venom to spread more quickly into the bloodstream. Following a bite, the primary concern is to slow blood flow between the bite area and the heart. Relax the victim in order to slow their heart rate and immobilize the affected limb (use a splint if available) at a level below the heart. Apply a snug bandage – not a tourniquet – above the wound toward the heart. Wash the wound with soapy water. Seek medical aid immediately.

TURTLES

Both of these species have cranky temperaments and, when threatened, can amputate a finger or toe with a quick bite.

Snapping Turtle
Chelydra serpentina To 18 in. (45 cm)
Note large head, knobby shell and long tail. Found throughout the eastern U.S. Its southeastern cousin, the alligator snapping turtle (*Macroclemys temminckii*) is up to 26 in. (65 cm) long and can weigh over 220 lbs. (100 kg).

Softshell Turtle
Apalone spp.
To 18 in. (45 cm)
Shell is soft and leathery. Has a long neck and sharp jaws. 3 North American species.

VENOMOUS LIZARDS

Small reptiles have scaly skin, toothy jaws and claws. 2 North American subspecies.

Gila Monster
Heloderma suspectum
To 2 ft. (60 cm)
Has beady skin and a striped tail. A shy, retiring species that only bites when provoked. When it bites, it clamps down with a pitbull-like grip and grinds its venom into its victim. Venom is highly toxic.

CROCODILIANS

Large reptiles have armor-plated skin and huge toothy jaws. 3 North American species.

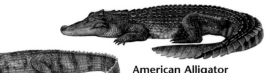

Spectacled Caiman
Caiman crocodilus To 8 ft. (2.4 m)
South American species has been introduced to south Florida waters.

American Alligator
Alligator mississippiensis
To 20 ft. (6 m)
Told by broad, rounded snout and blackish color. Ranges from North Carolina to Texas.

American Crocodile
Crocodylus acutus To 15 ft. (4.5 m)
Told by slender snout and gray-green color. Endangered species is found in extreme SE Florida.

BIRDS

Mute Swan
Cygnus olor To 5 ft. (1.5 m)
Orange bill has a black knob at the base. Nesting birds are very aggressive and have been known to break peoples' arms and legs; in one incident, a swan drowned a small child.

Deer
Odocoileus spp. To 7 ft. (2.1 m)
Have been known to attack humans without provocation and fight with sharp hooves and thrashing antlers. Considered the most dangerous North American animal, deer collide with approximately a million cars each year, killing 200 people and causing 100,000 injuries.

Collared Peccary (Javelina)
Pecari tajacu To 40 in. (1 m)
Pig-like southwestern species has black to gray fur, a white-to-yellowish collar and downward pointing tusks. Highly territorial and potentially harmful to humans. Packs have been known to be tree hunters and attempt to fell the tree by chewing away at the trunk.

Wild Hog
Sus scrofa To 6 ft. (1.8 m)
Has shaggy fur and prominent upward-pointing tusks. Color varies. Travels in packs and will attack humans if provoked.

MAMMAL BITES

The main danger of mammal bites is the risk of infection from tetanus or rabies. Seek medical attention immediately following a bite. Rabies is a life-threatening disease that is untreatable without the vaccine. While almost any wild or domestic mammal can get rabies, the most common carriers in North America are bats, dogs, raccoons, skunks, cats, foxes and coyotes. Rabies is usually transmitted by a bite or scratch. If wounded by a potentially rabid animal, let the wound bleed to help cleanse it, then thoroughly wash the wound with soap and water then seek medical attention. If possible, the animal should be killed and brought in for an autopsy.

Black Bear
Ursus americanus To 6 ft. (1.8 m)
Coat color typically ranges from black to cinnamon. An estimated 800,000 black bears occur throughout much of North America. They are responsible for the majority of bear attacks.

Grizzly Bear
Ursus arctos horribilis To 7 ft. (2.1 m)
Large brownish bear has a prominent shoulder hump and a 'dished' face. Approximately 25,000 grizzlies are found in mountainous regions of northwestern North America. Very unpredictable and dangerous when threatened, they will also feed on humans when hungry.

BEAR AWARENESS

To avoid bear contact, make loud noises when hiking (singing, talking loudly). Avoid carcasses and putrid smelling areas since these could be bear food caches. If you see a bear in the distance, make a wide detour downwind of the bear. If you encounter a bear, do not run since this may trigger an attack. Make yourself appear as large as possible and back away while talking in an audible, low voice. If a bear charges, hold your ground since it may bluff a charge and veer off at the last second. If the bear makes physical contact, fall face-down on the ground, clasp your hands behind your head and play dead. Resistance at this point will only provoke the bear. Be as still as possible until the bear relents. If the bear continues the attack, it is trying to eat you. Fight back and punch it in the nose and eyes.